Published in 2005 by
The Original Double Red Ltd
The Old School, Thorn Lane
Goxhill, N. Lincs
DN19 7JE. England

Tel: +44 (0)1469 531416
Fax: +44 (0)1469 531888
www.doublered.co.uk

ISBN 0-9534420-3-9

Photography: Double Red
James Wright
Gareth Harford
Sue Ward
David 'Chippy' Wood
Keith Lock
All images © Double Red

Project Manager
Sue Ward

Picture Research
Gareth Harford
Sue Ward

Picture Editors
James Wright
Sue Ward

Contributing Editor
Larry Carter

Design & Layout
Double Red & The Ark Design

Origination & Printing
The Ark Design & Print
Tel 0113 256 8712

Special Thanks to:
The organisers and sponsors involved in the British Superbike Series, especially
DORNA and MCRCB Events, whose dedication and commitment makes the Bennetts
British Superbike Championship the strongest domestic Championship in the World.
Every single person involved in the organisation and running of the Championship
whose often difficult jobs go un-noticed and un-rewarded... they know who they
are... medics, marshals, press officers, journalists, tv crews, truck drivers, mechanics,
chefs, cleaners, hospitality crews, commentators etc and not least, the riders, who
make the Bennetts British Superbike Championship the amazing spectacle it is.

Results and statistics
MST Timing

Contents

Foreword by Stuart Higgs

"Every bike has a lot of speed in it.
The trick is getting the speed out of it!"

Foreword
Seeing Red Vol 3 2005

The conclusion of the 2005 Bennetts British Superbike Championship marks the end of the second year of the series being run under the auspices of MCRCB-Events, together with our commercial partner Dorna UK. It's no coincidence that the Championship has grown significantly in this period. Since 2004, this new era of stability and confidence has, in turn stimulated the competitors, teams, circuits and the industry. The resulting quality and quantity of the teams and riders contesting the British Championship across all classes has been truly world class.

This years BSB Championship was billed as the strongest ever, with the highest ever permanent entry from the widest range of nations on the best equipment ever provided. My fear just before round one was, would it live up to all its pre season hype, as all the other major motorcycle Championships looked set for a season of domination by one rider?

Despite Ryuichi Kiyonari's best efforts to be 'Rossi-esque', the Championship was a fascinating encounter, as the pendulum swung between three of the best Superbike riders in the world. It was a story divided into three distinct parts. First there was the early domination by Kiyonari, in the opening rounds claiming four victories before his opponents had drawn a breath. Part two saw Michael Rutter take advantage of his team mates' Mallory Park misfortune and steadily build what, at one stage looked to be a certain Championship winning margin. Then the final third saw Gregorio Lavilla tenaciously claw back the advantage, along with a second wind from Kiyo. In the end, the best Championship to date went down to the wire with the ultimate contest between the best and most consistent two riders of the season, as I always hoped it would.

It was also a high spot watching Tommy Hill claim his maiden premier class victory and Leon Haslam consolidating his position as a serious championship contender. Bubbling away in Supersport was a new generation ready to graduate with the likes of Leon Camier, Craig Jones, Cal Crutchlow and Tom Sykes. We can now say with confidence that the British drought of GP success will soon be over, especially with the stunning array of talent being nurtured in the 125GP class.

Of course, working inside the sport makes it easy to be biased and self proclaiming, which is why it was extremely encouraging to see that the Daily Telegraph recently rated the British Superbike Championship as the highest entertainment value sport of all when debating the current downturn in the attractiveness of the Football Premier League. This accolade is richly deserved, due in no small part to the commitment and effort from all the individuals and parties that make up the BSB show, which is first class. I congratulate everyone on the delivery of a successful 2005 season.

So until April 2006 comes around and we do it all again, sit back and recall the all the drama and excitement of an epic season, captured so spectacularly, as always by Double Red.

Stuart Higgs
Series Director
MCRCB-Events

Gregorio Lavilla
Airwaves Ducati

For a rider to come to a championship he's unfamiliar with, on circuits he's never even seen before and win races and score rostrums with consummate ease speaks volumes about the likeable and quietly spoken rider from Tarragona. Quite simply Lavilla is world class and that has shone through beyond any doubt this season. People said the days of the vee twin Ducati were finished but Lavilla has made a mockery out of that and WSB's loss was very much BSB's gain for the cosmopolitan Spaniard. Whether he stays in the UK or not is another matter but Greg won't struggle to find a ride for 2006.

Ryuichi Kiyonari
HM Plant Honda

Kiyo's BSB debut experience last year wasn't a smooth ride in any shape or form and to some extent, 2005 wasn't either although at the start of the season, the Japanese rider looked invincible. Clearing off and winning the opening four races, he was brought back down to earth with a bang at Mallory when a nasty injury put him out of the next two rounds. If he hadn't missed those two rounds who knows .Once he learned how to mix it up with those that were prepared to rough him up, Kiyo showed his true class. Again it could be he'll be plying his trade on different shores next season but over these past two seasons, he's been a pleasure to behold.

Michael Rutter
HM Plant Honda

Any rider that leads such a competitive championship for seven rounds doesn't do so because he's a bad rider and as far as Rutter is concerned, he's one of the very best. His three round losing streak which netted him only 28 points in six rides (compared to Lavilla's 125 and Kiyonari's 110) and was typical of Rutter and his seeming inability to string together a championship challenge. But there were other issues which the public weren't aware of such as broken collarbones, ribs and a new front tyre which he struggled to adapt to.

Leon Haslam
Airwaves Ducati

As a former 500cc GP racer and WSB contender, 'The Pocket Rocket' could be forgiven for thinking that a move back to BSB would have been a step backwards and some would agree. But the imponderable in the equation was his team, and GSE Racing are no mugs when it comes to putting out competitive bikes. Once reacquainted with the circuits, Haslam was a constant thorn in the sides of the leading runners and but for a couple of indiscretions, could have been a major championship challenger this season. He wants to stay in BSB next season and if he does, he's a potential champion.

Glen Richards
Hawk Kawasaki

The Hawk Kawasaki isn't the best funded motorcycle on the grid, but what the bike lacks, then the Hinckley-based Aussie makes up for with talent and aggression in abundance. The superb double podium at Mallory was Glen Richards to a tee. When the chips are down and the team needs a result, good old GR comes up trumps. He ran with the leaders for many races and but for a broken collarbone at Snetterton, he could have been challenging even higher up the points table.

Dean Thomas
Hawk Kawasaki

The move to the extremely professional and well turned out Hawk Kawasaki team was very successful for the ex-Australian Supersport champion, 29 year old Yorkshire based Australian Dean 'Bam Bam' Thomas. Not only was he the only rider in the top ten to score points in every round, he also improved on last year's performance by moving up the championship ladder eventually finishing in sixth position. Undoubtedly a tremendous achievement for any rider making the transition from the Italian V-Twin to a Japanese four.

Karl Harris
www.honda-racing.co.uk

Karl 'Bomber' Harris's, year started strongly and petered off during mid season. Despite having some big crashes, he bounced back from all of them, and his form over Cadwell's mountain was more Supercross than Superbike. Harris is certainly one to watch out for next year, and he's not afraid to get physical if the situation requires him to.

Gary Mason
Stobart Honda

Mason joined the former Championship winning team run by Paul Bird, this time running the Stobart Hondas. The switch from Yamaha to Honda was to prove the right move for Mason, he didn't tear any trees up, but put in some consistent performances. He's had some difficult years, and although he shows he has the potential to be fast, he needs to start stringing together some podium performances.

Michael Laverty
Stobart Honda

Having not turned a wheel in the premier class before Brands Hatch, not much was expected of the young Ulsterman as this season was to be very much a learning year for him. A big crash at Brands Hatch in round one knocked his fragile confidence even further and just three points in the opening four races told the story. As soon as the Stobart team downsized to two riders (with Jeremy McWilliams getting injured), Laverty's results improved to the point where he was a regular podium finisher until a big crash at Silverstone set him back. Another future star shining brightly on BSB's horizon.

John Reynolds
Rizla Suzuki

A broken leg of the magnitude that the defending champion suffered in pre-season testing would have been enough to keep most racers out for the rest of the year but not JR. He rode less than six weeks later and posted a pair of top tens. Some said it was to keep Lavilla off the bike and given his success at Airwaves Ducati, it could have been a smart move by Reynolds. His end of season performances reminded everyone, as if they needed it, that a fit JR is a competitive JR. You simply don't lose class but another big off at Brands led to him announcing the end of an illustrious career.

HM Plant
Honda
Racing

HM Plant Honda

Michael Rutter and Ryuichi Kiyonari
Honda CBR1000RR Fireblade
HRC Race Team Manager: Tadayuki Okada

Having played themselves in during 2004, the factory backed 'Blades were proving to be the dominant force in the early stages of BSB 2005 but as soon as the other teams got up to speed, there was a noticeable chink in the HRC armoury and the title that looked to be theirs by rights looked decidedly dodgy going into the final couple of races. The only bikes on Michelin rubber once again, lessons were learned from the 2004 season and any advantage they had in the early part of the season was soon negated by the Dunlop-shod competition as they hounded the pre-season favourites.

Having retained the services of TT and North West 200 winner Michael Rutter, who had led the championship from round three at Mallory up until his Cadwell disaster, along with Japanese ace Ryuichi Kiyonari who returned from winning the Suzuka 8 Hour race, the nucleus of the team that finished runners up to Reynolds and Suzuki last season remained for 2005.

Despite never winning a single domestic championship to date, thirty-two year-old Rutter's mid season form was once again his nemesis although in fairness, he struggled with the new profile front tyre which led to a number of crashes and resulting injuries. Twenty-two year-old 'Kiyo' from Saitama, struggled mid season last year but ended up blitzing the opposition at the final round and continued that form with victories in the opening four races this season to lead the title chase. However, a heavy smash at Mallory ruled him out of rounds three and four and Rutter grabbed the initiative by taking over at the top with a superb double of his own.

Once again, the HRC operation was overseen by former 250cc and 500cc Grand Prix winner Tady Okada and the ever present Neil Tuxworth.

Airwaves Ducati

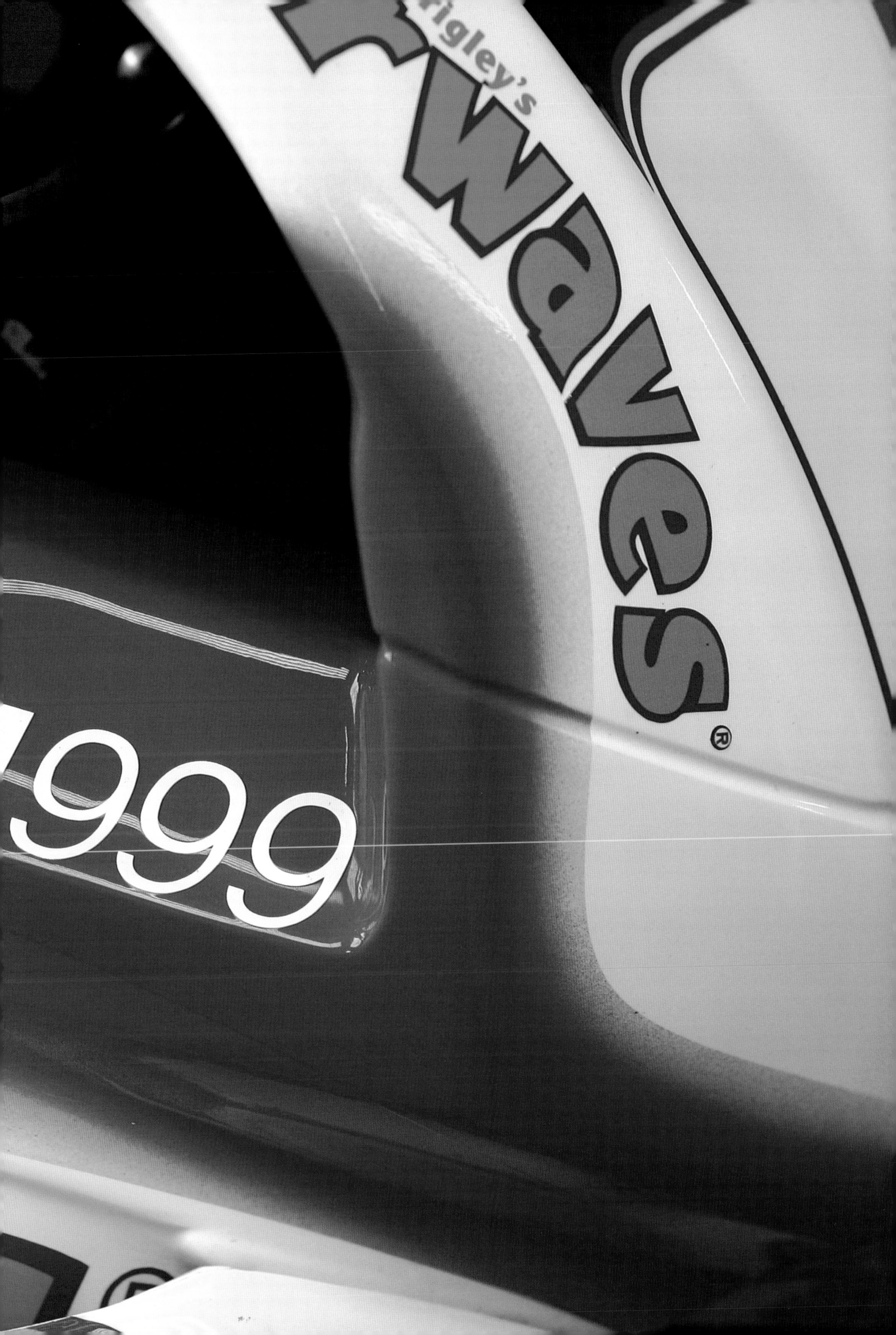
rigley's
Waves®
999

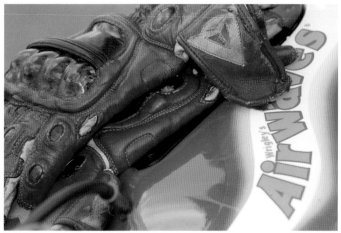

Airwaves Ducati

Leon Haslam and Gregorio Lavilla
Ducati 999 F04
Team Principal: Darrell Healey
Team Manager: Colin Wright

The team that breeds world champions came back home to race after they curtailed their World Superbike Championship action at the end of 2003 and right from the outset, what a stir they caused.

Originally having signed James Haydon to ride alongside ex GP and WSB star Leon Haslam, Haydon was injured during pre-season testing which necessitated the team to draft in 'super-sub' Gregorio Lavilla for the start of the 2005 series.

Such was the Spaniard's performance (he finished on the podium in all four races to lie second in the championship after Thruxton), it caused a major dilemma for the team when Haydon was declared fit again. Without the infrastructure to run a three rider team, Haydon took the unprecedented and magnanimous step of offering to 'withdraw' from the team in order to let Lavilla concentrate on the championship for the remainder of the season.

And what an inspired decision it was with Lavilla's performances eclipsing many for most of the season. The very fact that the former WSB rider hadn't seen most of the circuits let alone ridden on them spoke volumes about his ability and the subsequent square off for the title was even more ironic given HM Plant, Honda's main sponsor, used to sponsor the GSE team in WSB!

The 2005 version of GSE Racing featured largely the same backroom staff as in previous years, headed up by owner and Team Principal Darrell Healey. Running the ex Fila factory Ducatis of James Toseland and Regis Laconi, disciplinarian Team Manager Colin Wright once again looked after the racing operations of the double British Championship winning team on their return to the 13-round series with the full blessing and support of Ducati Corse and title sponsorship in the shape of Wrigley's Airwaves brand.

Having secured two previous crowns in the British Championship, with Troy Bayliss in 1999 and Neil Hodgson in 2000, the credentials of the GSE Racing operation were unquestionable, as the results on the track this season proved.

Hawk Kawasaki

Hawk Kawasaki

Glen Richards and Dean Thomas
Kawasaki ZX-10R
Team Principal: Stuart Hicken

Stuart Hicken runs a very tight-knit yet capable team and with a year's development behind the ZX-10R, it was no surprise that the pair of Aussies in the shape of Glen Richards and Dean Thomas were knocking on the door for the most part.

A broken collarbone wrecked Richards' outside title chances although he was a regular podium visitor and ran at the front in plenty of races and whilst Thomas could qualify well, he had difficulty in making the results stick in the actual races.

Richards took a pair of second places at the team's home track of Mallory Park at the start of the season as they continued to put one over on some of their more illustrious rivals while Thomas was the only rider in BSB to score points in all races such was his consistency.

Hicken and his faithful squad have stated that they would like to dip a toe in the World Superbike arena at some point and given the professionalism they have exuded over the past few years at BSB, they'd be very much at home in that paddock.

Rizla Suzuki

www.suzuki.co.uk

IZLA

S ben

British Superbike C

Rizla Suzuki

John Reynolds and James Haydon
Suzuki GSXR1000K5
Team Manager: Robert Wicks

A number of rostrum finishes for defending champion John Reynolds towards the latter part of the season salvaged something which by Rizla Suzuki's very high standards, was a disastrous campaign. The team that was dealt a hammer blow on the eve of the season with the news of Reynolds' broken leg in testing and despite a brave effort to race at Brands Hatch in the opening round where he scored two superb ninth places, Reynolds suffered afterwards with the injury and had to admit defeat at both Thruxton and Mallory. He sat out the next two meetings in order to rest the injured limb. Many riders would have called it a day for the season but not Reynolds, his British bulldog fighting spirit epitomises everything about the man.

Having parted company with Scott Smart straight after the Croft round former Foggy Petronas rider James Haydon – who deputised admirably for Reynolds at Oulton Park and Mondello – got the call to arms and secured the ride for the remainder of the season. He promptly celebrated by falling off in race one at Knockhill and doing likewise at Snetterton! A class act whose career has been in the doldrums in recent times, the supply of a competitive machine was just the tonic that Haydon needed but for whatever reason, he struggled more than he should have.

Team owner Paul Denning leaving to ply his trade as boss of the Suzuki's Moto GP team meant leaving former WSB marketing guru Robert Wicks in charge. Wicks was ably assisted by any number of staff including Niall Mackenzie who as usual combines his role in the team with his journalistic duties.

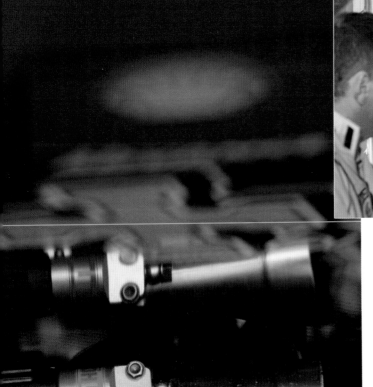

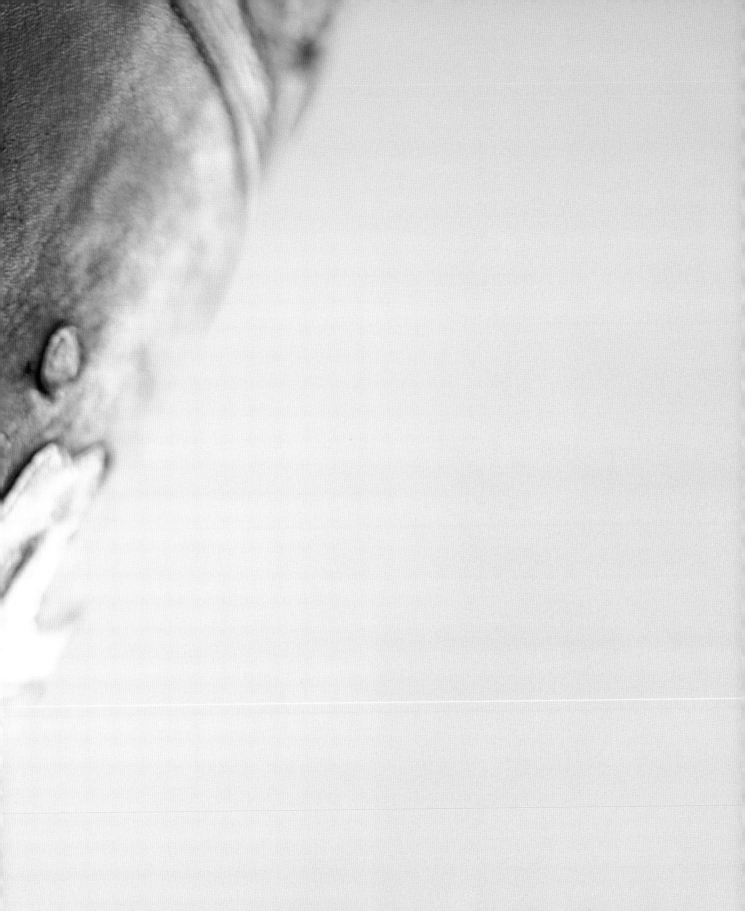

Virgin Mobile
Samsung Yamaha

Virgin Mobile
Samsung Yamaha

Tommy Hill, Sean Emmett and Richard Wren.
Yamaha YZF-R1
Team Principal: Rob McElnea

Now in the sixth year of association with Sir Richard Branson's telecommunications empire, Rob McElnea's team once again combined youth with experience but for the second year in a row, early season injuries to their mercurial team leader scuppered their bid for the title.

With Sean Emmett's absence, the role of lead rider was entrusted to former Virgin Yamaha R6 Cup winner Tommy Hill, and how he has matured this season. If it hadn't been for a run of wretched luck at the start of the year, the twenty year-old would surely have racked up a rostrum finish sooner than he did but when the race victory came at Cadwell, the relief and emotion were plain for all to see in both rider and team.

Having won races for the team on his previous shift back in 2002, Emmett was tipped for success on the radical 'Big Bang' engined R1s (affectionately dubbed 'The Pig' by Emmett) but was laid up following surgery on an injured elbow in mid season. After an inauspicious performance at both Cadwell and Oulton, Emmett's lack of fitness proved to be his undoing as he struggled for the most part.

Emmett's enforced absence meant James Haydon deputised for one meeting (Croft) and Aussie Dan Stauffer came in for Knockhill although they chose not to field a replacement at Snetterton. As a result, rookie of the year last season Hill, and fellow R6 Cup winner Richard Wren were thrust into the limelight and acquitted themselves well, Hill winning at the non championship Castle Combe meeting and Wren scoring points as the season progressed.

Stobart Honda

Stobart Honda

Jeremy McWilliams, Gary Mason and Michael Laverty
Honda CBR1000RR Fireblade
Team Owner: Paul Bird

Flamboyant rally driving millionaire Paul Bird looked to have
pulled off one of the coups of the series in recent years by
landing GP racer Jeremy McWilliams as part of another three
rider team but as far as the forty-one year-old Ulsterman is
concerned, it's been a season to forget.

As MonsterMob Ducati, the team won the BSB title in 2002
with the late Steve Hislop before repeating the feat a year later
in the hands of Shakey Byrne and Bird saw McWilliams as the
man to recapture the crown. But the veteran of twelve years
on the continental circus which comprised of 186 GP's
crashed out in the opening two rounds sustaining a niggling
shoulder injury which scuppered his chances.

McWilliams underwent extensive therapy on his right
shoulder but still had only 50 percent strength and movement
although he did surprise everyone (including Birdy) when he
took to the grid aboard the Proton for the Czech GP. Bird
wasn't best pleased and promptly fell out with McWilliams
who didn't return until the final round at Brands Hatch.

Fellow countryman Michael Laverty has astounded many in
the paddock and trackside with his performances this season
meaning he's rapidly become the find of the series. However, a
horror smash at Silverstone saw the youngster sustain some
nasty internal injuries which forced him to miss some rounds in
the latter part of the season while team mate Gary Mason put
in some consistent finishes throughout.

Vivaldi Racing

Vivaldi Racing

Scott Smart, Ben Wilson and Tristan Palmer
Kawasaki ZX-10R
Team Owner: Tony Gee

After a successful debut season in the National
Superstock Championship, Britain's newest team
made an impressive leap into BSB with
promising Superstock stars Ben Wilson and
Tristan Palmer. Both riders had previous BSB
experience and made a lasting impression – as
well as tasting the occasional tarmac – this term.
Palmer led a BSB race outright at Mallory and
'Spud Missile' Wilson gained his best results of
the season at Snetterton as Suzuki cast-off
Scott Smart joined the team at Knockhill.
Smart's nightmare season continued when he
crashed out after tangling with Sean Emmett
at Silverstone and despite bravely trying to ride
at Cadwell and Oulton, had to admit defeat
through injury.

Red Bull Honda

Jonathan Rea
Honda CBR1000RR Fireblade
Manager: Havier Beltran

With Neil Tuxworth and Havier Beltran co-ordinating the efforts of the independently liveried and Dunlop as opposed to Michelin shod bikes, many didn't expect a great deal of Red Bull rookie Jonathan Rea in his debut superbike season, especially after missing half of the 2004 season with a broken leg.

But after a couple of rounds to play himself in, the talented Ulsterman exploded onto the scene in dramatic fashion when he became the youngest ever rider to set a BSB pole position at Mondello and went from strength to strength.

www.honda-racing.co.uk

Karl Harris
Honda CBR1000RR Fireblade
Team Manager: Havier Beltran

After winning back-to-back British Supersport crowns, the mercurial Harris signed a deal to move up to the premier class having last ridden in it for Suzuki during an injury-ravaged 2002 season. As a satellite offshoot of the main HRC effort, and with backing from BLD and www.honda-racing.co.uk, complete with striking orange and red livery, Harris, a former European Superstock Champion and renowned hard man of racing, endured a season of mixed fortunes which saw him on the podium twice at Oulton but also suffer egg-beaters of crashes at Mallory, Silverstone and Croft, the latter leaving him with three broken ribs.

   With ex WSB crew chief Tom Larsen in his corner, the transition was not as tough as it could have been and although Harris is a man of few words, he is a class act who gave a damn good account of himself in what has been the toughest ever assembled field in BSB history.

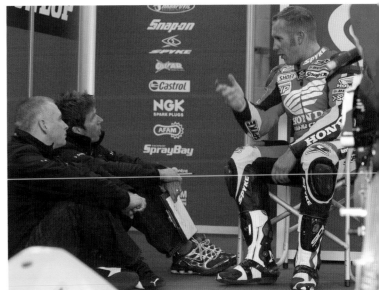

AIM Racing

Chris Burns & Les Shand
Yamaha YZF-R1
Team Owner: Alistair Flanagan

Another team changing name as well as machinery for 2005 was Alistair Flanagan's ETI Ducati concern which became AIM Racing. Some reshuffling in the team saw the departure of original rider and double 2005 TT winner John McGuinness and in came ex MotoGP rider Chris Burns but the Geordie didn't experience the best of luck after joining the team at Snetterton. A broken foot at Castle Combe and hand at Cadwell led to Scotsman Les Shand take over the R1.

Hydrex Honda

Kieran Clarke and Steve Plater
Honda CBR1000RR Fireblade
Team Owners: Colin Appleyard & Shaun Muir

Another rider to suffer more than his fair share of injuries in 2004, Clarke this year teamed up with former racer Shaun Muir and long term backer Colin Appleyard Racing in another independent Honda concern. Muir has had success in recent years with Honda and Clarke was hoping to reap the benefits after a year aboard a semi-factory Yamaha with Appleyard last term. After parting with Sendo, former BSB winner Steve Plater was drafted into the team at Snetterton and rewarded them with a fifth place.

At the final round of the season at Brands Hatch, Steve went on to give the team its first rostrum finish when he out-gunned both the factory Hondas, to claim a fine third.

Nvidia GR Motorsport

Dennis Hobbs & Sheridan Morais
Yamaha YZF-R1
Team Owners: Brent Gladwin & Tony Robinson

After a season of 125 racing the Sheffield based outfit made the step up to the superbike class racing with twenty-two year-old Dennis Hobbs at the helm. Running ex Yamaha France factory bikes, the Brent Gladwin team struggled with the Pirelli tyres in the opening rounds and Hobbs, who broke his neck last season, struggled to recapture his form following a broken wrist during practice at Oulton Park which ruled him out for three rounds. He did however score points at the WSB meeting at Brands Hatch but crashed out at Cadwell and missed the races as a result. Diminutive South African Sheridan Morais deputised when Hobbs was injured but didn't feature strongly.

Jentin Racing

Luke Quigley
Yamaha YZF-R1
Team Owner: Bernie Toleman

The Superbike Cup champions of last year dipped a cautious toe into the 'works' ranks as well as keeping a presence in the 'privateers' championship until reverting to a single rider team. Having split with Dean Ellison, former Supersport runner Luke Quigley came on board and improved as the season progressed.

WORDS ARE NOT ENOUGH.

D208RR

ROUND
01
Brands Hatch
28th March

Top left: Kiyo started the season where he aimed to finish it… at the front of the pack

Bottom right: Karl Harris and Glen Richards had a few close scraps just outside the podium positions

Right: ETI returned as AIM Racing with John McGuinness

Bottom: JR raced at Brands despite sustaining multiple fractures to his right leg during pre-season testing only 37 days earlier

Above: Lavilla was happy with his 2nd and 3rd places standing in for the injured James Haydon

Bottom left: JR had a boot specially made by Alpinestars to support his injury

Below: 'Jezza' returned to BSB after several years of MotoGP action

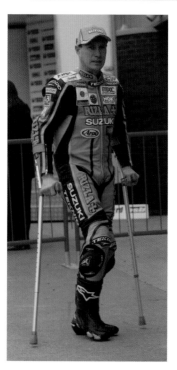

Brands Hatch
28th March

The strongest field ever assembled in British Superbike history converged on Brands Hatch over Easter with no less than 35 bikes taking to the grid with every major manufacturer represented.

Before a wheel had been turned at Brands, the drama had begun to unfold with defending champion John Reynolds breaking his leg in five places in pre-season testing aboard the Rizla Suzuki. No one gave him a chance of riding just 37 days later but the old warhorse proved his doubters wrong and posted a pair of top ten finishes which was simply amazing.

James Haydon wasn't so fortunate – a broken hand putting paid to his debut aboard the Airwaves-backed GSE Ducati. Super-sub Spaniard Gregorio Lavilla stepped in, permanently as it turned out.

'Pocket Rocket' Leon Haslam set pole for the returning GSE team but

after being fired out of the saddle in race one, wrenching his delicate wrist in the process, he couldn't manage a podium so it was down to Lavilla to take the plaudits with a second and a third place.

But up front there was no stopping the factory backed HM Plant Honda of Japanese star Ryuichi Kiyonari who obliterated the opposition in both races. He won the first race by ten seconds and the second one by five after rolling it off in the latter stages – and proved the year's apprenticeship that he and the Michelin tyres served in 2004 was a sound investment.

Aussie Glen Richards climbed the podium in the opening race for the Hawk Kawasaki team after fending off pre-season title favourite Michael Rutter to make it an historic all-foreign podium, although Englishman Rutter redressed the balance with a second place behind his team mate in race two.

Sean Emmett bravely battled against a nasty elbow injury sustained in qualifying to claim a brace of top five placings and MotoGP refugee Jeremy McWilliams crashed out of race two after tangling with a backmarker. Both riders would suffer lasting repercussions as a result of those injuries as the season progressed…

But the question on everyone's lips was who, if anyone could catch Kiyo. On this showing, the championship was his and it was just one round old. The rest were already playing catch up…

Points (after round one)

1	Kiyonari	50
2	Lavilla	36
3	Rutter	33
4	Richards	25
5	Emmett	22
6	Harris	20

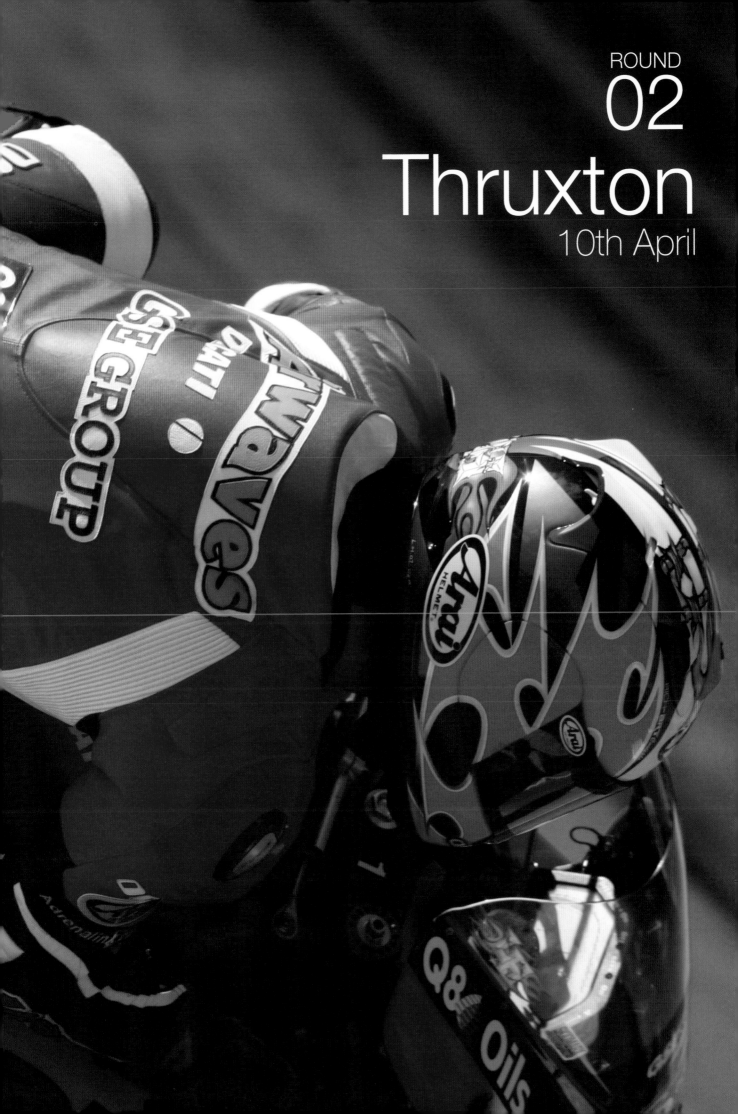

Bottom left: Emmett continued his strong start to the season

Above: Richards and Harris continued their close racing

Left: Rutter tucks everything in over Thruxton's high kerbs

Top: Scott Smart (88) chases Dean Thomas on the Hawk Kawasaki that kick-started 'Smartarse's BSB career in 2004

Bottom left: Tommy Hill puts on his 'race face' and if this style (pictured right) is the result, then it certainly works

Far right: Leon Haslam has the support of his lovely girlfriend while Dennis Hobbs has Brent Gladwin!

Above: JR struggled with the fast and bumpy Thruxton but the pain was eventually too much to endure

Left: McWilliams all dressed up and nowhere to go

Thruxton
10th April

On his Brands showing, it would have taken a brave person to bet against Ryuichi Kiyonari repeating his performance at a bright, albeit breezy Thruxton but the enigmatic Orient Express proved once again that nothing is certain in this life when he crashed at high speed during the final throes of qualifying. Various rumours emanated from the HRC pit, including a potential broken ankle and whilst that news, if indeed true, wasn't what everyone wanted, it might at least give the rest a chance.

Rutter grabbed the pole ahead of Haslam, Emmett and Harris with Kiyo languishing down on row two, but come race day, Kiyonari hobbled to his machine to take to the grid and any hopes the opposition had of racking up some easy points were soon diminished.

Notwithstanding a hairline fracture in his foot and no mean amount of bruising, the twenty-three year-old more or less repeated his Brands performance with a resounding win in race one, followed up by a much closer affair in race two to make it a maximum four wins from four starts. Team mate Rutter and Airwaves Ducati's Greg Lavilla shared the other rostrum places in both races, the latter being announced as a permanent fixture in the team for the remainder of the year, despite a declaration from Haydon that he'd be fit for the next round in a couple of weeks time.

Emmett, Haslam and Richards were again impressive but already the cracks were beginning to show in one or two teams. Reynolds battled against the pain and the cold before succumbing to his injuries and team mate Smart was struggling with the set up on his K5.

The Sendo Kawasakis of Steve Plater and Jon Kirkham were a mile off the pace, as indeed were the Stobart Hondas whose main title hope McWilliams crashed out for the second meeting in succession, further injuring his already damaged shoulder.

As the teams left Thruxton with Kiyonari's advantage already at 28 points, the Japanese rider's domination of the series seemed inevitable. If he could win races injured as well as fit, then it was only a matter of time before he became the first Japanese winner of the toughest domestic series in the world.

Points (after round two)

1	Kiyonari	100
2	Lavilla	72
3	Rutter	69
4	Emmett	46
5	Richards	43
6	Harris	38

MALLORY PARK 50
50 Years of Motorsport Glory

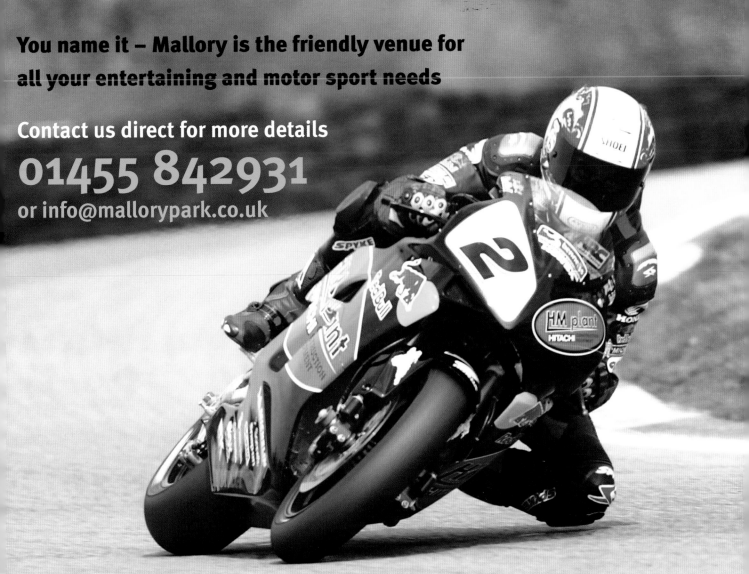

The friendly circuit celebrates 50 glorious years in 2006

Mallory is the complete venue

- Corporate activities • Race day hospitality
- Off road activities • Track days
- Weddings, dinners, parties

You name it – Mallory is the friendly venue for all your entertaining and motor sport needs

Contact us direct for more details

01455 842931
or info@mallorypark.co.uk

ROUND
03
Mallory Park
24th April

Facing page
Far left: Kiyo slides his HM Plant
Honda into the hairpin and (bottom
right) McWilliams' misfortune
continues

This page
Bottom left: Richards stuffs his
Hawk Kawasaki up the inside of
Rutter's HM Plant Honda into the
hairpin

Top: If Kiyo's not sliding into the hairpin, he's "stoppying"…and then it all went horribly wrong as he crashed out of the lead in race one (sequence)

Right: Kieran Clarke takes a tight line through the bus stop

Bottom: Rutter took full advantage at his local circuit and left with maximum 50 points!

Far right: Thomas scrapes his arm on the wall at the infamous hairpin

Mallory Park
24th April

BSB returned to 'The Friendly Circuit' after a year's absence with a promise of good things around the Leicestershire speedbowl, but as it transpired, it will be remembered mostly for all the wrong reasons.

For the first time in BSB history, there was either a pace car intervention or a race stoppage in every single race – which eventually led to the final Superstock race being postponed. A number of the crashes responsible for these interruptions were horrendous looking to say the least, and the fortunate fact is, that everyone (just about) came away unscathed.

Tommy Hill ripped his arm open and Danny Beaumont sustained back injuries in the same Devil's Elbow smash and although both needed hospital treatment, they were back in action within a round or two. Karl Harris and Greg Lavilla collided at 130mph on the exit of Gerrards and both were lucky to escape serious injury. Series leader and pole setter Kiyonari was another such rider who ended the weekend's action in the medical centre after an horrific crash in the opening race when he slammed head first into the barriers under braking for the new Edwina's chicane. Mercifully, he was okay as it turned out but the concussion he suffered ruled him out of Mallory and also jeopardised his chances the following week at Oulton due to the designated 'eight day' ruling which applies in the case of head injuries.

Rutter took maximum advantage at his local circuit amidst the carnage and recorded his first double since Croft last summer to move to the head of the championship table, while another local rider Glen Richards enjoyed the best BSB performance of his career, finishing as runner-up in both races on the Hawk Kawasaki.

The Airwaves Ducatis of Leon Haslam and the battered and bruised Greg Lavilla took a rostrum apiece, with perhaps the only rider in the red and white team gear not celebrating being a certain James Haydon who had, according to the official statement 'stood down in the best interests of the team'.

Rizla Suzuki took the decision at Mallory to withdraw the brave but struggling Reynolds from the series until such time as his injuries had healed and Stobart Honda team boss Paul Bird threatened that unless results improved, his three rider team would be downscaled. McWilliams, the last British winner of a solo GP at Assen in 2001, struggled with his arm injury again and as a result was placed on the sick list in order to allow it the necessary time to recover.

The meeting also heralded the first of the newly conceived 'sprint races' as a result of the second BSB stoppage. No longer a 'two-part' race scenario, the riders contested the remaining laps as a straight race in its own right and at the end of the twelve-lapper, just twenty seconds separated the first fifteen riders home.

Points (after round three)

1	Rutter	119
2	Kiyonari	100
3	Lavilla	88
4	Richards	83
5	Emmett	65
6	Haslam	62

Oulton Park
2nd May

Bottom left: Leon Haslam doesn't have to start his own machine but uses the starter as a prop.

Bottom centre: James Haydon was back… on a Rizla Suzuki having 'stood down' from the Airwaves Ducati Team. This time he deputised for JR who had decided to rest his still injured leg.

Above: Lavilla was already in the thick of things…

Right: …but had no problem using every millimetre of suspension travel under braking

Above: Sean Emmett's early season form started to tail off.

Bottom left: Steve Platers X-rays showed a piece of metal embedded in his skull – the legacy of a car crash some years ago. (There had to be a reason for Plater's behavior!!)

Top right: Harris continues to show strong form.

Oulton Park
2nd May

With Kiyonari still recovering from his Mallory mauling a week previous, it was a case of everyone else trying to exploit the former MotoGP star's absence and to steal a march on the title.

Michael Rutter continued where he left off at Mallory by setting pole position and the most successful BSB rider around the Cheshire circuit was looking good to increase his and HM Plant Honda's domination of the championship.

But one thing you can always rely on to upset the apple cart is the good old British Bank Holiday weather and as the bright sunshine of race day morning gave way to thicker clouds; it was only a matter of time before the rain rolled in.

Race one went the distance in the dry but not before drama unfolded in the pits as Leon Haslam came in after the warm-up lap. The Airwaves Ducati rider dropped his F04 in haste to change to his spare bike and with no small amount of leniency from the pit lane marshal, was allowed to join mid pack whereby he battled his way up to fourth.

Rutter took an easy win to make it seven out of seven for Honda ahead of Lavilla with Karl Harris grabbing a debut superbike podium for Honda GB, but as rain started to fall on the grid for race two, tyre choice was again going to be critical.

Having made the right tyre choice and despite no mean amount of fairing bashing, Haslam slithered and slid to victory on a drying track ahead of Rutter with Harris again third, and for the first time in eight races, three Brits stood on the podium.

James Haydon, drafted in to ride the Rizla Suzuki in place of the resting Reynolds, came home fourth ahead of Frenchman Julien Da Costa (MSS Discovery Kawasaki) whilst Lavilla struggled on a disintegrating tyre and finished out of the points leaving Rutter with an increased advantage of 56 points.

Scott Smart again struggled all weekend and Virgin Mobile boss Rob McElnea was vociferously critical of Sean Emmett who was not at his usual best retiring in race one and claiming 11th in race two.

Points (after round four):

1	Rutter	164
2	Lavilla	108
3	Richards	104
4	Kiyonari	100
5	Haslam	100
6	Harris	80

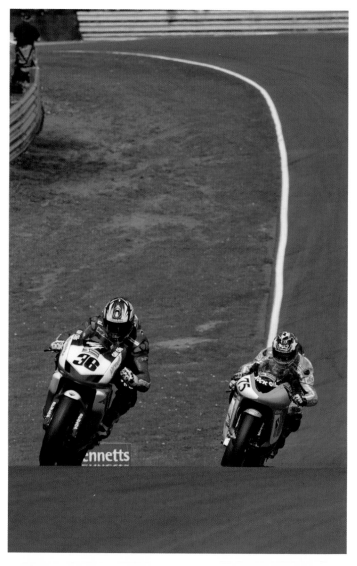

ROUND
05
Mondello Park
15th May

Top left: Kiyo was back – picking up where he had left off with a win in race one

Top right: Three goes into two on lap one

Centre: Jonathan Rea had become the youngest 'pole sitter' in BSB history but crashed his Red Bull Honda out of the first race before turn one

Top left: Plater turns on the style while Hill keeps it smooth and neat

Above: Richards takes a tight line while… **left:** Nick Medd struggled on the ARCO Kawasaki due to the niggling shoulder injury he sustained in 2004

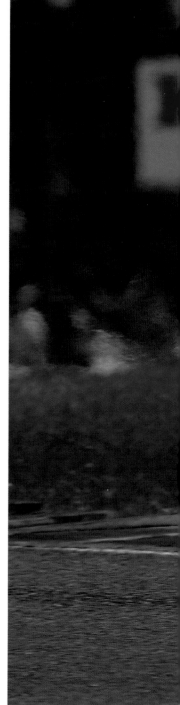

Left: John McGuinness had his head down but still struggled

Right: The lead pack were evenly stretched

Mondello Park
15th May

The annual trip across the Irish Sea saw the teams descend on the impressive venue to the south west of Dublin where once again Irish eyes were smiling in more ways than one.

Not only did the sun shine for the third year in succession but two youngsters from the Emerald Isle, albeit the Northern sector, emerged as serious contenders to the established superbike order in the shape of Honda riders Jonathan Rea and Michael Laverty.

Rea, son of TT winner Johnny, in his rookie season in the big bike class after just three years on the tarmac, took a sensational pole position aboard the Red Bull backed Fireblade as he headed the top fourteen riders, all of who were under the lap record in qualifying.

Sadly for the teenager, his race lasted just one corner as he was punted off in the opening leg. He also slid out of contention in race two but at least he'd made his mark. So too did Laverty aboard the Stobart bike who harried and chased the leaders throughout the two races, eventually claiming a fourth position for his efforts. It was the start of something special for the young Ulsterman.

Kiyonari, back from injury, started where he left off at Thruxton by clearing off and winning from the front in race one ahead of Rutter and Lavilla but it was in the second race that Kiyo got his come-uppance as BSB 2005 got physical. Realising that when he's given the chance to get ahead, the Honda rider usually clears off, both Airwaves boys Haslam and Lavilla pack-hunted the Japanese star before stitching him up on the very last corner to relegate him to third.

Kiyonari wasn't happy, and neither was the team given some wayward comments from the TV commentators, but it did provide the likeable Lavilla with an historic first win in the series for both himself and Spain. After the race he suggested that he'd perhaps have a celebratory Guinness or two. It was also the first time that anything other than a Michelin-shod Honda had won a race in 2005 which in itself gave Dunlop and Ducati something to cheer about.

Championship leader Rutter could only manage fifth in the second race, muscled out by BSB rookie Laverty, meaning his lead had been cut to 46 points. Haydon, in his final ride (for now) aboard the Suzuki threw away their first potential podium while McWilliams conceded defeat to his injuries declaring that he wouldn't ride again until he was fixed. Sean Emmett likewise, after recording his 200th BSB appearance decided his elbow wasn't healing as it should and sought medical advice. It turned out he'd been riding since round one with it broken…

Points (after round five)

1	Rutter	195
2	Lavilla	149
3	Kiyonari	141
4	Haslam	120
5	Richards	114
6	Harris	79

www.shell.com/advance

Shell Advance

Supporting the 2005 British Superbike Championship

Shell Lubricants

Top left and below: Kiyo briefly considered a second career as a photographer for Double Red then quickly decided he would need to spend more time in the gym

Left centre: Richards and Kiyo get up close and personal at 130mph as do Lavilla and Plater (below left)

Above: Lavilla first time out at Croft had another strong showing – as did Rutter (centre)

Below: Hill pulls in to retire after being torpedoed during the pace car intervention

Right: JR was back at Croft but still struggled

Far right: Rutter's HRC Honda shows Jonathan Rea who's the boss

Bottom right: Lavilla bullies Kiyonari into the hairpin

Croft
5th June

After scoring a double on the series' first ever visit to North Yorkshire in 2004, Michael Rutter was hoping for a repeat dose and set about it in fine fashion by posting fastest time during qualifying to start from pole for the third time this year. Rather embarrassingly for the official Suzuki team, privateer James Buckingham planted his private GSXR in front of both Rizla men on the grid.

Once again the weather played its part as the intermittent rain caused chaos with both teams and organisers alike with precipitation falling on the back part of the circuit with the front remaining dry.

Race one saw Kiyonari spring from the blocks like the proverbial scalded cat and romp to a victory, whilst the others were still in their slumber it seemed as both Rutter and Lavilla again had no answer to him. Karl Harris' race was over on the warm up lap with ignition failure while Jon Kirkham was on the operating table getting repairs done to a smashed finger sustained in the previous day's qualifying.

Race two saw the rain intervene half way through which brought out the red flags and riders were faced with a sprint race over 14 laps. What ensued pertained to be one of the races of the season. Harris' misery had already been completed when he crashed at Tower breaking some ribs and Laverty's bike suffered fuelling problems when he was again running strong.

Seven riders battled it out lap upon lap with Lavilla eventually gaining his second win of the season ahead of Rutter with Kiyonari again beaten into third after another mauling. The resurgent Steve Plater aboard the Sendo Kawasaki crashed out on the last lap after James Haydon, this time riding the Virgin Yamaha in place of the now injured Sean Emmett, had done a couple of laps earlier.

Haslam slid off and poor Tommy Hill's luck went from bad to worse when he was torpedoed by another rider during a pace car intervention. The end result was that Rutter held onto his series lead going into the second half of the season with his tenth podium in eleven races.

Points (after round six)

1	Rutter	235
2	Lavilla	190
3	Kiyonari	182
4	Richards	138
5	Haslam	130
6	Harris	102

don't just take our word for it!

x-spirit

kagayama TC5

xr1000

alloy TC1

raid2

destiny

SHOEI®

for your nearest stockist call
01384 410 384
www.shoei.feridax.com

ROUND
07
Knockhill
26th June

Far left: James Haydon was back on the Rizla Suzuki – this time as replacement for Scott Smart who had changed camps going to the Vivaldi Kawasaki Team

Left: Lavilla and Haslam might be team mates, but it didn't stop them toughing it out!

Top left: Considering he prefers flat open circuits, Kiyo didn't do too badly at Knockhill with two wins!

Bottom left: Just let me squeeze through says Hayden

Below: Scott Smart had a change of leathers from the Rizla blue to the Vivaldi maroon

Above: GR leads JR

Top left: Lavilla battles to hold off Kieran Clarke on the Hydrex Honda as…

Centre: …Jonathan Rea tries to hold off a charging Dean Thomas

Knockhill
26th June

For what seemed to be the first time in living memory, the sun actually shone at a BSB round at Knockhill and as significant as that was, it paled into obscurity given Ryuichi Kiyonari's dominance on the Scottish mountainside.

Pole position, two race wins and a new lap record (eventually bettered marginally by team mate Rutter) saw the Honda rider reassert his authority on the series following his couple of races in the doldrums (if two wins and two podiums in four races can be considered that...)

Like at so many tracks the year previous, Kiyonari had no form and no suggestion that he'd be the dominant force, but to win both races by a cumulative twenty seconds spoke volumes of his desire to get his championship challenge back on track. No longer did he want to risk getting roughed-up in the pack, he did what he does best and that's to win both races from the front.

Rutter again had no answer and openly admitted he didn't know what he had to do to beat his team mate, so did the next best thing and settled for a brace of second places as he applied the damage limitation exercise that weekend. The factory Hondas were a class apart leaving the rest to chase their ever-increasing shadows.

One rider who did just that was Michael Laverty who gave the Stobart team their first and his inaugural podium with a calculated ride in leg one which he followed up with a fourth in race two having seen off a concerted Airwaves Ducati challenge. Lavilla, who has a residence in Scotland, responded with a podium in race two to keep the championship front runners within his reach.

James Haydon, replacing the departed Scott Smart at Rizla Suzuki, celebrated his call up with a crash whilst Smart found refuge in the fledgling Vivaldi team aboard a Kawasaki he was much more familiar with although his results were still not impressive. John Reynolds was back and somewhere like fighting fit which was reflected in a pair of top seven finishes.

Rather perversely, Rutter just lost two points of his lead and it remained at 43 points as both Kiyonari and Lavilla vied for the right to chase him. The meeting also marked the non-appearance of the Sendo Kawasaki team due to financial reasons leaving Steve Plater and Jon Kirkham bikeless.

Points (after round seven)

1	Rutter	275
2	Kiyonari	232
3	Lavilla	216
4	Richards	160
5	Haslam	152
6	Harris	115

Far left and left: Rutter and Kiyonari were both trying hard – tough guy Rutter with one dislocated and one broken collarbone from a practice crash!

Bottom left: Emmett's X-rays prove why he'd struggled!

Left: Tommy Hill had his best result of the season to date

Snetterton
10th July

The championship very nearly took an unexpected twist as competitors and officials alike reeled in the shock of the London bombings in the run up to the meeting. An innocuous looking highside coming out of Russell's chicane slapped Michael Rutter hard into the ground and despite 'The Blade' walking back to his garage to take to his spare bike, all appeared not well with the championship leader.

Undeterred, Rutter battled on in some apparent discomfort and posted third fastest time behind pole setter Leon Haslam and HM Plant Honda team mate Ryuichi Kiyonari.

After an early challenge, Kiyo did his disappearing act at the front in race one and cleared off leaving the pack to swallow up the ailing Rutter who ended up in a lowly fifth, his championship lead under extreme threat, as he claimed his quickshifter wasn't working. Haslam came home second and John Reynolds, the outgoing champion, gave Rizla Suzuki something to cheer about with his and his team's first podium in fifteen long races after both Lavilla and Laverty had retired.

Rutter admitted he needed to do something about Kiyonari as it appeared the Japanese rider had the championship lead at his mercy.

Haslam's 'Duke' expired early on leaving Rutter in command but another dust-up involving a number of riders saw Kiyonari crash out on lap six at the Esses handing the initiative back to Rutter. Lavilla eventually came through to win ahead of the resurgent Laverty with Rutter trailing home in third and adding to his points tally. But as the riders headed for the podium, Honda team boss Neil Tuxworth revealed that Rutter had broken a collarbone in that practice smash and damaged the other one too.

That put Rutter's performance into perspective and he was rewarded somewhat by increasing his series lead by a mere but all important two points.

Glen Richards was another rider in the wars having broken a collarbone in practice too and Jonathan Rea was hospitalised for the weekend with internal injuries following his heavy practice crash.

Better news included Steve Plater gaining a competitive ride aboard the spare Hydrex Honda as team mate to Kieran Clarke and he impressed with a pair of stunning rides whilst ex MotoGP rider Chris Burns replaced TT winner John McGuinness on the AIM Yamaha.

Young guns Tommy Hill (Virgin Mobile Samsung Yamaha) and Ben Wilson (Vivaldi Kawasaki) posted their best results of the season too in the near-tropical temperatures of sunny Norfolk as the series went into a five week summer recess.

At least the walking wounded had time to heal and Rutter, Richards as well as Emmett were expected to contest the next round.

Points (after round eight)

1	Rutter	302
2	Kiyonari	257
3	Lavilla	241
4	Haslam	172
5	Richards	160
6	Harris	125

28 Bikes, 28 Riders, 12 races

One big fat prize...
A years contract with Team Virgin Mobile Samsung in the BSB

This is The Virgin Mobile Cup and they are

THE NATURAL BORN RACERS

Screened on **Five** January 06

Silverstone

21st August

Top left: Laverty stretches before race one… his body was to need all the flexibility possible when he was hit by Harris' crashing bike

Top of this page: Dean 'Bam Bam' Thomas got a good start but was unable to translate it into a podium placing

Above right: Karl Harris couldn't realise why he was getting so much attention on the grid

Bottom right: 150mph… 150mm gap

Far right: The 'Blade' glistens through 'Bridge'.

Below: TT winner John McGuinness was on the Vitrans Honda

Left: The Hawk Kawasakis stuck together

Below: Rutter gets off to a good start

Right: With no team orders, Haslam and Lavilla battled tooth and nail

Silverstone
21st August

After a five week break, the BSB circus rolled back into action at the plush surroundings of Silverstone with the walking wounded from Snetterton healed for the most part, although there was talk that Michael Rutter had been nursing some broken ribs.

Fresh from victory at the Suzuka 8 hour race, Ryuichi Kiyonari obliterated the lap record during qualifying to place the HM Plant Honda on pole alongside his team mate Michael Rutter but as the bikes left the grid for race one, little did anyone know what drama lay ahead.

First of all a big smash involving Michael Laverty, Karl Harris and guest WSB rider Ben Bostrom brought out the red flags and then in the restart, Kiyonari slid off the Honda early on at the low speed chicane. It handed the advantage to Rutter who was comfortably in second place behind Spaniard Gregorio Lavilla when inexplicably, he crashed at the same spot as Kiyonari on the penultimate lap.

Airwaves Ducati took the 1-2 with Kiyo clawing back to claim 8th and Rutter managed to salvage a solitary point in 15th after a one handed ride to the flag courtesy of a broken handlebar.

Race two saw Kiyonari claim maximum points ahead of the two Ducatis with Rutter languishing down in fourth and hanging onto the series lead albeit by a reduced margin of 26 points. But the smiles on the faces of the HRC top brass who had jetted in for the meeting were not as wide as they had hoped, as the Italian-Spanish equation of Ducati and Lavilla were now a major force just four points adrift of the Japanese rider.

John Reynolds inherited third in race one thanks to the Honda self-destruction but the defending British Champion crashed out in race two adding to Rizla Suzuki's woes in a day which was strewn with a plethora of pace cars and red flags.

The soap opera which is the Bennetts British Superbike Championship had started a new storyline and the twists and turns had only just started…

Points (after round nine)

1	Rutter	316
2	Kiyonari	290
3	Lavilla	286
4	Haslam	208
5	Richards	182
6	Harris	145

blackhorse
MOTORCYCLE FINANCE
Unleash the Horsepower

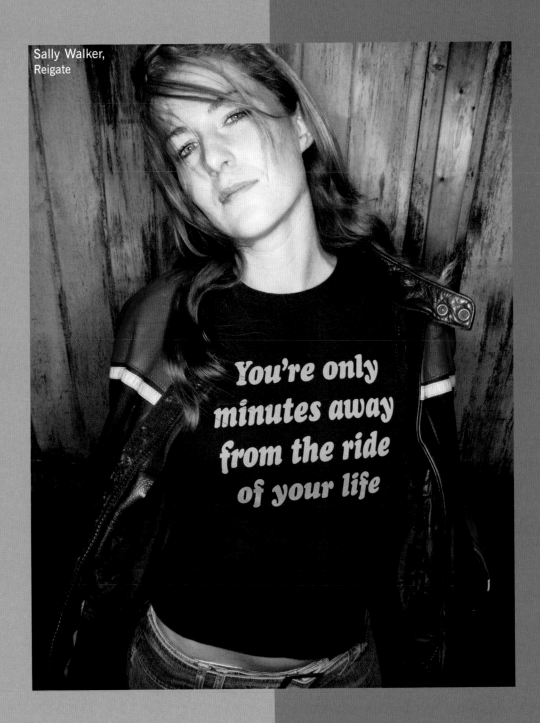

Sally Walker,
Reigate

You're only minutes away from the ride of your life

Fast finance from your dealer

If you want it – have it. Getting the bike of your dreams is simple
if you use Black Horse Motorcycle Finance. No messing with forms.
No wasting time waiting for funds to clear. And with our Lloyds TSB
backing, plus competitive rates, you can be sure you've got a great
deal. Finance without the fuss. Minutes after walking into one of our
dealerships you could be out on the open road. We're not here to
come between you and a beautiful new relationship.

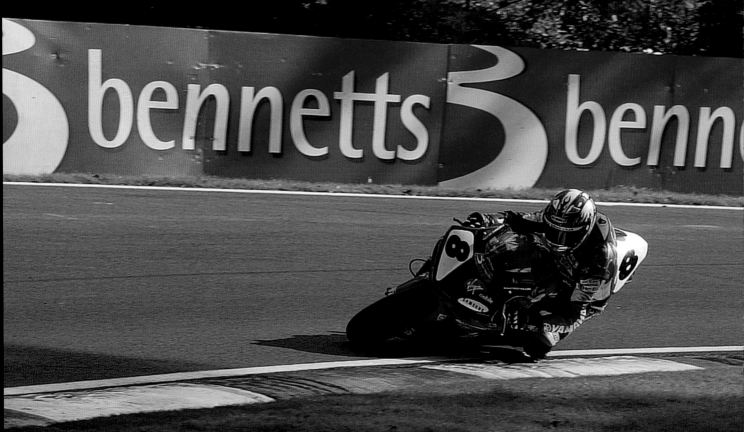

ROUND
10
Cadwell Park
29th August

ts 5 bennetts 5 bennetts

The trees and undulations of Cadwell Park
always give a different perspective for the riders
as they blast through the shadows

Top left: Tommy Hill kept a close eye on Haslam and Lavilla before they tripped each other up… Hill took his first BSB win

Centre left: Karl 'Bomber' Harris flies over the mountain

Top: Jonathan Rea puts his off-road experience
to good use and out-jumps even Harris

Cadwell Park
29th August

Cadwell Park is renowned for two things every August Bank Holiday and once again this year it came up trumps. A massive crowd always descends on the Lincolnshire valley and nigh on 40,000 souls ventured along with camp sites full two days beforehand. It also throws up more surprises than any other circuit and yet again, no one could have written the script.

The two Airwaves Ducatis taking each other out in race one, Michael Rutter throwing away the championship lead in every literal sense of the word in race two and Virgin Yamaha gaining their first win of the year with starlet Tommy Hill's first trip to the top of the BSB Podium. It couldn't have been more dramatic.

The factory Hondas struggled all through qualifying, a fact not helped by Rutter crashing at Charlies, but not so Lavilla and Haslam on the Airwaves Dukes who were a class apart all weekend. But it very nearly ended in disaster on the final lap of race one when a kamikaze move by Haslam put himself and his team mate on the grass at Park Corner handing victory on a plate to Hill who was holding a menacing third. The thousands on the bankings gasped in awe as they watched on the big screen as Lavilla recovered to take second with Haslam fifth. Glen Richards sneaked in to take his first podium since Mallory as Rutter limped home in eighth, three places behind Kiyonari.

Race two saw a revitalised Rutter up at the front and looking to maximise his advantage over the slow-starting Kiyonari but once again the two Ducatis upped the pace, and Rutter had no answer as Kiyo cut a swathe through the field. Eventually, Rutter pushed too hard and down he went at high speed rounding Chris Curve, beating himself up in the process although luckily without major injury. Again the crowd gasped as the black leathered 'Blade' appeared on screen seemingly down and out.

Kiyonari continued his ascendancy to claim third spot, but all eyes were focussed on the battle at the front to see if there would be a repeat of the race one antics. Needless to say, there wasn't although in some people's eyes, Haslam taking the win and with it, the five extra points was tantamount to slapping his team mate in the face.

No team orders are fine but if it ends up costing Ducati the championship then who knows the consequences? The end result was that Lavilla left Cadwell two points to the good ahead of the unfortunate Rutter with Kiyonari, seven points further back in third.

So it was a day of firsts at Cadwell. The first time the Spaniard had led the series all season and the first time Rutter had relinquished it since Mallory and also the first time that an emotional Tommy Hill had heard the British national anthem for himself in front of thousands overlooking the podium.

Points (after round ten)

1	Lavilla	326
2	Rutter	324
3	Kiyonari	317
4	Haslam	243
5	Richards	199
6	Harris	169

Top left: Kiyonari and Lavilla battled like crazy.... Anyone who thought Kiyo couldn't cope when things get physical were proved very wrong as paint was exchanged and elbows used!

Bottom left: The same goes for the rest of the pack

Left: Dean Thomas in the thick of the action

Right: Kiyonari could not have concentrated harder if he had tried

Far left: The boards tell the story…

Centre left: …as does Rutter's look of disgust.

Left: Lavilla was initially given the win but the timekeepers gave it to Kiyo by .004 of a second – no wonder he looks disillusioned!

Oulton Park
11th September

Just when people thought the championship couldn't throw up any more surprises, along came the second visit of the year to the picturesque Oulton Park with all still very much to play for.

Michael Rutter's last win in the championship came at the same track some 14 races earlier and if anyone needed a change in fortune, it was 'The Blade'. But qualifying went badly for him once again and but for a last lap effort, his HM Plant Honda team mate Ryuichi Kiyonari would have joined him on row three of the grid. Series leader Gregorio Lavilla sat ominously on pole position aboard his Airwaves Ducati, his team mate Haslam having won at Oulton earlier in the season.

Kiyonari tried to stamp his trademark authority by clearing off in race one but Lavilla hunted him down and just for good measure took a rejuvenated John Reynolds aboard the Rizla Suzuki along with him. The slow-starting Haslam couldn't track them down in time and that's the way they stayed as they crossed the line with Rutter a distant 10th complaining of rear brake problems.

Oulton has a habit of throwing up repeat results and so it happened again in race two but again no one could have predicted the drama. Kiyonari and Lavilla started to pull a gap on Reynolds but cutting a swathe through the pack was Rutter, stung into action as he saw his championship disappearing.

Lap four and Rutter was inside the top six and hunting down the leaders when he clipped the kerb at Britten's and down he went for the third time in as many meetings. Rutter, the crowd nor the astonished onlookers in pit lane could believe it and to all intents and purposes, it was down to a two horse race for the title

Into the final lap and still Lavilla and Kiyonari were trading blows, barging elbows and covering moves as they dived for the line. Lavilla looked to have secured his first win in six races as the timing monitors gave the win to him by the narrowest of margins. But just as the Airwaves team were starting their celebrations, the screens changed and Kiyonari was declared the winner!

An anxious wait then ensued as officials studied the replays and when the result was declared in the Japanese rider's favour, a whoop of joy from the normally reserved team was significant in itself, as indeed was Kiyo's one point lead going into the penultimate round. It was the first time he'd led the series since Thruxton whereby he'd won the opening four rounds of the series.

Points (after round eleven)

1	Kiyonari	367
2	Lavilla	366
3	Rutter	330
4	Haslam	269
5	Richards	218
6	Harris	188

ROUND

12

Donington Park

25th September

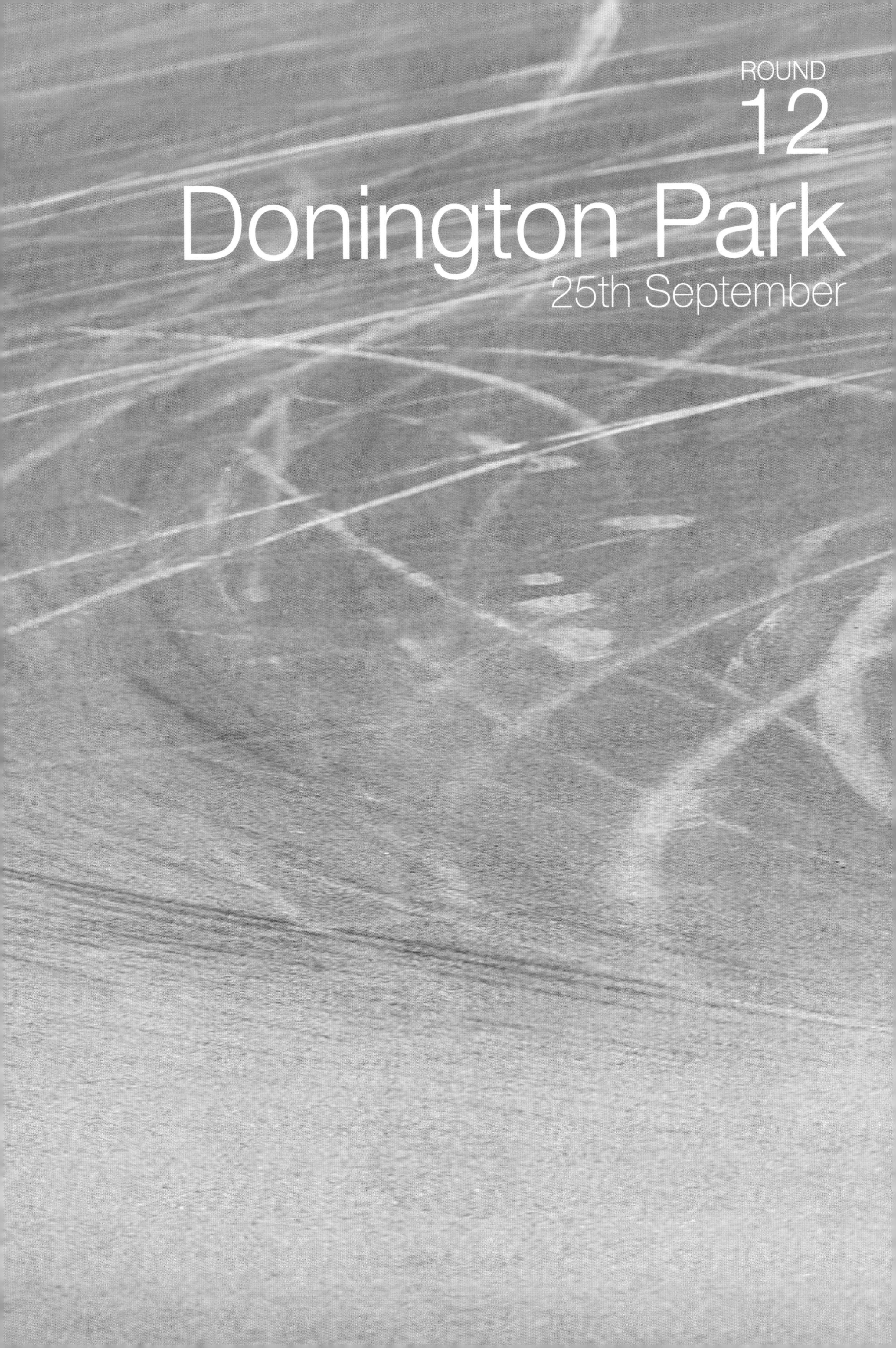

Top: Part of the plan? Haslam's start is not quite straight as he squeezes out the HM Plant Hondas, leaving his team mate acres of space

Right: No matter how hard he tried, Kiyo couldn't catch Lavilla

Above: The ups and downs of racing – JR knows them both better than most

Below left: James Haydon kicks up the dust

Below right: Kiyo spins it up out of the Melbourne Loop

Donington Park
25th September

A timely first double of the season for himself and for the Airwaves Ducati team saw Greg Lavilla clasp one hand firmly on the BSB title after more drama was played out at the penultimate round, this time courtesy of the weather at an autumnal Donington Park.

A second successive pole and talk of a revolutionary new Dunlop tyre was just what the opposition didn't want but the HM Plant Honda pairing of championship rival Ryuichi Kiyonari and now a somewhat title outsider in the shape of Michael Rutter looked to be making a fist of things as they sat on the front row alongside the other Airwaves interloper, Leon Haslam.

Notwithstanding both Lavilla and Kiyonari had tipped off in practice, raceday dawned bright and after a race-long duel, Kiyo had to give second best to the Spaniard as the Michelins – so long with advantages around Donington Park – had no answer to the F04's Dunlops. Haslam came home in a distant third, unable to help his team mate.

Rutter's title aspirations finally expired as he trailed home in sixth, his cause not helped by a nagging shoulder injury sustained in a Cadwell Park smash which effectively ended his bid.

So the tussling trio became a dicing duo as for the first time ever, the destiny of the series was to go to Spain or Japan. Once again in race two, Lavilla stamped his class on the field. A torrent worthy of the GP had soaked the track as well as the entire population of Donington and although a dry line had appeared following the Supersport race, it was narrow to say the least. Kiyonari struggled and was up and down the leaderboard like a yo-yo as the two Dukes headed off into the distance whilst throughout the field, riders were unloading with gay abandon.

Lavilla held his nerve to chalk up his sixth victory of the season as the onlooking Ducati Corse contingent of Paolo Ciabatti and Davide Tardozzi

doffed their imaginary caps in admiration, with Haslam riding to perfection and boxing off second place.

Kiyonari's disappointment was evident as he stood alone in parc ferme and he, like Honda, could feel the title that looked to be theirs by rights earlier this season, slowly slipping away. As the Spanish anthem rang out over the Airwaves, Kiyo nor Lavilla cast a look or a congratulatory hand in either direction. The respect is mutual but the pain of defeat is unimaginable. Thirteen points was Lavilla's advantage leaving round twelve meaning the destiny of the title was very much in his, and not Kiyonari's, own hands…

Points (after round twelve)

1	Lavilla	416
2	Kiyonari	403
3	Rutter	353
4	Haslam	305
5	Richards	231
6	Harris	195

Honda Ron Haslam Race School

If you are looking for a biking experience you'll never forget the Ron Haslam Race School is for you.

The Race School, run by racing legend 'Rocket' Ron Haslam is the premier european race school offering 3 course options

On Track:
£159

Introduction to riding Performance bikes.
Using CBR125F and CB500
Young riders Welcome (12 yrs+)

Premier:
£249

Using CBR600RR
Detailed briefings 1 instructor to 2 pupils.
3 Track sessions

Elite:
£349

Using CBR1000RR Fireblade.
One to one instruction and with full Data logging.
4 Track sessions.

Tel: 01332 883323
Fax: 01332 780814

All your equipment is supplied!, Bikes, Leathers, Helmets, Gloves, Boots and Instruction

All you need to do is book it!

www.haslamraceschool.com
e: enquiries@haslamraceschool.com

ROUND

13

Brands Hatch

9th October

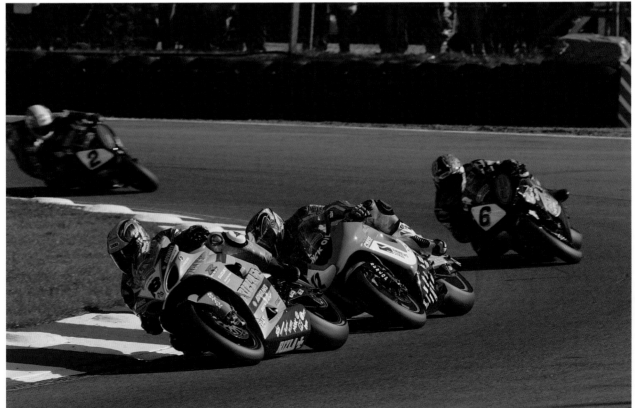

Right: Tristan Palmer treats his Kawasaki like his Vivaldi sponsors treat their potatoes, and leaves it firmly-planted in the Paddock Hill gravel trap

Left: Mason was keen to impress and backs it in at Druids

Above: The low sun and long autumnal shadows give the riders yet another problem to overcome

Far left: James Haydon was unable to convert his fantastic qualifying performance into a race win

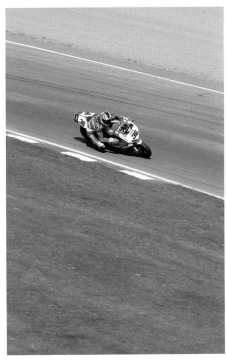

Facing page

Top left: Haslam rode 'shotgun' for Lavilla, making regular checks on the opposition behind

This page

Top: Leon Haslam literally came out of the shadows this season with some fantastic performances

Above left: Plater on the Hydrex Honda lines up Kiyonari on the HRC Blade for a pass

Left: The Pack charges into Druids

Facing page
Top centre: The pit boards tell the story

Centre left: Talk about different styles… both seem effective!

This page
Formation flying… team mates just can't help sticking together

Brands Hatch
9th October

In the final analysis, it was almost a formality. The two Airwaves Ducatis were comfortably on the front row of the grid, the HM Plant Hondas were back on the third row and off the pace. Qualifying had given the GSE team the edge and they were in no mood to let it slip in the double race final showdown at Brands Hatch.

Alright, James Haydon, who had started the season as one of their riders, had shattered the lap record to claim his first ever Superbike pole start aboard the Rizla Suzuki but as the action began for real, it was Leon Haslam on the charge, hotly pursued by Gregorio Lavilla.

The Spanish rider, cheered on by his travelling fans, who had journeyed to the Kent circuit from his home town of Tarragona, roared him on and on the fifth lap going into Druids, as Haslam ran wide, Lavilla was through, and en-route to the victory that virtually assured him of the crown.

Ryuichi Kiyonari, his only rival in the title stakes, was back in fourth place, unable to make any real impact on the proceedings as he ran adrift of Haydon and the maturing Haslam who was doing a great job riding 'shotgun' a third of a second down on his team mate.

That success meant Lavilla needed only a single point from the second race to secure his first major crown. There was no easing off. He shattered the outright lap record as he finished in second place, yards behind the commanding Haslam, to take the champion's trophy.

"Fantastic – it is a great feeling but I did not expect to be standing here at the start of the season. My thanks to the team and to Dunlop for the tyres. My bike has been consistent, very good. After the summer break we raced on circuits I knew and started winning regularly, taking points back from the Hondas.

"I think you say 'mission complete' – it has been a great year and we have finished it well," smiled the champion who ironically had begun the campaign without a contract, merely the 'stand-in' for two rounds as Haydon recovered from a hand injury. He had packed the early season points, making the bike his, and then a strong second showing of six wins and five second placings proved just champion.

Kiyonari, was again fourth, this time finishing adrift of Steve Plater riding the Hydrex Honda. The Japanese rider will be back in 2006 with the factory Honda team, hoping to make it a case of third time lucky in the title stakes, while the GSE team will be aiming to take the crown for a fourth time.

Haslam, who proved a real force to be reckoned with confirmed prior to the last round that he would be riding for them: "I can hardly wait for the start of the season – I can't thank the team enough and to have two 1–2 finishes in each of the final two races is just brilliant."

Final championship standings:

1	Lavilla	461
2	Kiyonari	429
3	Rutter	371
4	Haslam	350
5	Richards	241
6	Thomas	198

British Superbike
Championship Winners
oiled by Q8

2004 Rizla Suzuki | 2005 Airwaves Ducati

For those who don't believe in coincidence!

British
Superbike
Cup

Lanky West Country rider, James Buckingham followed in the footsteps of MotoGP stars Shakey Byrne and James Ellison by winning the supporting BSB Privateer's championship with consummate ease as it turned out.

With minimal backing and racking up the miles to and from every meeting, the twenty-one year-old proved the star of the field by taking a dozen victories in total aboard his Quay Garage Suzuki and with alarming regularity, embarrassed a number of the factory riders into the bargain.

Noticeable was his performance at Croft when he out-qualified both Rizla factory bikes in the shape of Scott Smart and John Reynolds; a fact not lost on the Crescent team hierarchy who promptly offered him a one-off deal to race JR's bike at the non-championship Castle Combe meeting whereby he plonked it firmly on the rostrum.

Indeed Buckingham was drafted into the factory squad again for the final round at Brands when Reynolds was injured in pre-event testing but with so little time to set up the machine, he had to settle for lower leaderboard placings.

Former National Champions Chris Martin (125) and Danny Beaumont (Superstock) took victories during the campaign, as did Ulsterman Marty Nutt and Scouser Steve Brogan but none could match the consistency of 'Big Bucks' who on his way to becoming the first champion crowned this season, racked up an amazing seven successive wins in the class.

British Supersport Championship

An overheating engine at the penultimate round for Leon Camier simply delayed the inevitable with the gangly Kent rider eventually wrapping up the title in clinical fashion at Brands Hatch.

Just needing a 12th place finish to secure the title (assuming main rival Craig Jones won), the former 125cc GP racer rode a calculated race into fifth place with Jones holding onto second position when the red flags came out due to a crash involving Pere Riba.

2005 was one of the closest and most dramatic Supersport seasons in recent years. All six leading protagonists were in with a shot of the title at various stages but injuries ended up costing Tom Sykes, Stuart Easton and Jay Vincent dearly.

Camier however remained cool following a couple of DNF's early in the season and despite

never claiming one pole position all season long, he proved the class act of the field when it mattered and is surely destined for a return to the World championship arena before too long.

Victories went the way of Vincent, Sykes, Easton, Riba and Cal Crutchlow as well as Camier although Jones never managed to top the rostrum.

The Supersport Cup went down to the very last round also and after the dropped rounds had been taken into account, it was Gary Johnson who claimed the title in dramatic fashion.

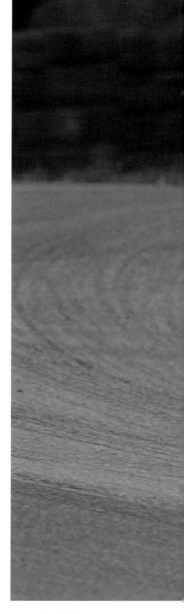

Metzeler National
Superstock Championship

What looked to be Aussie Paul Young's title by rights in mid season ended up being snatched from under his nose as Lee Jackson was crowned champion for 2005 in another dramatic finale.

Young won four out of five races between Mallory and Knockhill and finished second in the other to plant one hand on the crown but a dismal run of form and some bad luck conspired against him allowing Adrian Coates and Jackson to home in.

Coates and Jackson battled it out in superb fashion at the Brands curtain closer and both took turns to place their hands on the trophy at various stages throughout the race until Coates went down in a big way at Paddock Hill Bend leaving Jackson to cruise home with Youngy down the order.

Twice winner Andy Tinsley's season was curtailed mid season due to personal reasons and other victors included Ian Hutchinson who shocked the established order at Donington and Craig Fitzpatrick who took an inaugural win at Brands.

Peter Ward took the honours in the supporting National Superstock Cup after seeing the chequered flag first in 50 per cent of the races.

Virgin Mobile
Cup

Australian Billy McConnell won the dramatic penultimate championship round to claim the biggest prize in UK motorsport when he secured the Virgin Mobile Cup Championship in conditions that could best be described as extreme.

In only his first full season of British racing, the eighteen year-old saw off the considerable opposition to reserve his place in next season's British Championship Virgin Mobile Samsung Yamaha squad and in doing so, followed in the footsteps of Brit's Tommy Hill and Richard Wren as winners of the competition.

But it wasn't all plain sailing for the erstwhile series leader for the most part as a worrying mid season slump in form had the opposition baying at his door and threatening to claim this unique prize.

Along with fellow Aussies Brendan Roberts and David Anthony, the trio caused a stir both on and off the track and despite the best efforts of his fellow countrymen, 'Billy Whizz' had it under control.

Early season challengers in the shape of Ulsterman Ian Lowry and Dubliner Mark Pollock were soon dispensed with, while Englishmen Tommy Bridewell, Adam Jenkinson and Jon Boy Lee offered resistance at various stages throughout the season but a relative lack of consistency meant that they didn't trouble McConnell unduly.

McConnell's only misdemeanour was when he crashed out at Knockhill but with victories at Oulton and Croft as well as at Donington, plus a number of podium places, it proved he was a worthy recipient of the R1 berth:

"I really can't believe it, it's brilliant. I went to Donington knowing that I had to win but there were moments when I had visions of it going down to the wire at Brands. I would have been really disappointed with myself had I not won there but I just want to thank everyone, my family and the crew for all their support and hard work. Let's party!" said Billy afterwards.

The British 125 GP Championship

The only two-stroke offering on the menu went down to the wire in a classic winner-takes-all scenario which was a repetition of the same situation twelve months earlier when Christian Elkin emerged victorious from Donington.

Elkin, the early series pacesetter but who suffered a mid-season lull, was one of the three riders to go into the Brands finale with a chance of the title, as was Rob Guiver and teen sensation, James Westmoreland.

Guiver threatened to blow it by falling at the penultimate round at Donington throwing Westy and Elkin a lifeline but in a dramatic final round, mechanical failure – their only ones of the season – robbed both Guiver and Westmoreland of the title leaving Elkin to coast home to an easy victory and with it, his second successive 125cc title…

Other race winners this term included teenagers Kev Coghlan, Bradley Smith and Chris Jones.

Westmoreland took some consolation by taking the honours in the ACU Academy Cup as the talent of tomorrow came under close scrutiny from the bosses at DORNA, with a number of riders combining the British series with the illustrious Spanish Championship.

Chris Jones
Red Bull Rookie

Behind the scenes

2005 Bennetts British Superbike Championship
Points after final round

Rounds: R1–R2 Round 01 Brands Hatch Indy 28 March 2005 · R3–R4 Round 02 Thruxton 10 April 2005 · R5–R6 Round 03 Mallory Park 24 April 2005 · R7–R8 Round 04 Oulton Park 2 May 2005 · R9–R10 Round 05 Mondello Park 15 May 2005 · R11–R12 Round 06 Croft 5 June 2005 · R13–R14 Round 07 Knockhill 26 June 2005 · R15–R16 Round 08 Snetterton 10 July 2005 · R17–R18 Round 09 Silverstone 21 August 2005 · R19–R20 Round 10 Cadwell Park 29 August 2005 · R21–R22 Round 11 Oulton Park 11 September 2005 · R23–R24 Round 12 Donington Park 25 September 2005 · R25–R26 Round 13 Brands Hatch GP 9 October 2005

Name	Total	R1	R2	R3	R4	R5	R6	R7	R8	R9	R10	R11	R12	R13	R14	R15	R16	R17	R18	R19	R20	R21	R22	R23	R24	R25	R26
Gregorio LAVILLA (Ducati)	461	20	16	16	20		16	20		16	25	16	25	10	16	25		25	20	20	20	20	20	25	25	25	20
Ryuichi KIYONARI (Honda)	429	25	25	25	25					25	16	25	16	25	25	25		8	25	11	16	25	25	20	16	13	13
Michael RUTTER (Honda)	371	13	20	20	16	25	25	25	20	20	11	20	20	20	20	11	16	1	13	8		6		10	13	10	8
Leon HASLAM (Ducati)	350		13	13	9	16	11	13	25		20	10		11	11	20		20	16	10	25	13	13	16	20	20	25
Glen RICHARDS (Kawasaki)	241	16	9	7	11	20	20	11	10	10		11	13	13	9			11	11	16	1	11	8	13			11
Dean THOMAS (Kawasaki)	198	8	5	8	10	10	13	10	1	1	3	6	10	6	6	5	7	10	10	7	9	5	9	7	10	11	11
Karl HARRIS (Honda)	195	10	10	10	8		10	16	16	13	9					8	5	10		13	7	13	11	8	11	7	
Gary MASON (Honda)	174		6	4	3	8	9	9		8	7	7	11	7	3	8	8	9	9	5	6	7	7	6	9	9	9
John REYNOLDS (Suzuki)	139	7	7	2									4	9	10	16	13	16		4	8	16	16	11			
Michael LAVERTY (Honda)	129	1	1	1		9	7	3	6	10	13	13		16	13	20									6	5	5
James HAYDON (Suzuki)	126							8	13	6		8				8		13		6	8	9	10	10	11		16
Tommy HILL (Yamaha)	123	6	4	6							2			1	4	6	9	7	6	25	13	9	10	8			7
Steve PLATER (Honda)	111			3	6			5	9	2	5	5	9			9	11	5			7		6	5		8	16
Scott SMART (Kawasaki)	97		8	9		11	8	7		11	8	3	3	4		2	2							9	8	4	
Sean EMMETT (Yamaha)	94	11	11	11	13	13	6	5		9											3	3	5	3			1
Jonathan REA (Honda)	64	3		4		2	2	4	7		9				7			4	5						6	6	6
Ben WILSON (Kawasaki)	62	5	3	1			5	1	2	3	1	4			2	7	10			2		2		4	3	3	4
Kieran CLARKE (Honda)	41		5		1			6	8	5		8			2				1		3				2		
James BUCKINGHAM (Suzuki)	39	5		5	1							2			5				4	6	5	4	4	1			
Jeremy McWILLIAMS (Honda)	36	9			7					7	6																7
Tristan PALMER (Kawasaki)	28	2				3	3	3					1	3	1	3		2	2			1					
Danny BEAUMONT (Honda)	20	4				7											5			1							3
Steve BROGAN (Honda)	19		2			6						1	7		1								2				
Julien DA COSTA (Kawasaki)	13										11													2			
Jon KIRKHAM (Kawasaki)	12								4	4	4																
John McGUINNESS (Yamaha)	12		2			5	4															1					
Dennis HOBBS (Yamaha)	11						4							3	3												
Richard WREN (Yamaha)	11															4	4							3			
John LAVERTY (Honda)	8								2				6														
Chris MARTIN (Suzuki)	7														5						2						
Chris BURNS (Yamaha)	6																6										
Marty NUTT (Honda)	4									2														2			
Dean ELLISON (Honda)	4																							4			
Lee JACKSON (Kawasaki)	3																3										
Luke QUIGLEY (Yamaha)	1																							1			
David JOHNSON (Kawasaki)	1																										1

2005 British Superbike Cup
Points after final round

Name	Total	R1	R2	R3	R4	R5	R6	R7	R8	R9	R10	R11	R12	R13	R14	R15	R16	R17	R18	R19	R20	R21	R22	R23	R24	R25	R26
James BUCKINGHAM (Suzuki)	462	20	25	25			16	25	16	16	20	16	16	25	25	20	11	25	25	25	25	25	25	25	11		
Chris MARTIN (Suzuki)	352	13	16	13	13	13	20			25	9	11	20	13	16	25	13	11		16	20	13	13	20	13	13	13
Marty NUTT (Honda)	326		20		16	11	16	16	20	20	10	25			20		16		16	11	10	20	16	13	25	25	
Steve BROGAN (Honda)	288	10		20	25	20	25	20		11	16	20	25	20		16	10	20		20							
Malcolm ASHLEY (Kawasaki)	267	9	11					13	25	10	11		13	16	13	13	10	13	20	13	11			10	16	20	20
Danny BEAUMONT (Honda)	243	25			20		25			13	25	13					25			20	16			16	20	25	
Michael PENSAVALLE (Kaw)	172	11	13	11	10			11	13		13		11		11			10	13	16	11	9					
Gareth GLYNN (Yamaha)	63	16		16	11	10		10																			
Phil GILES (Suzuki)	43																							11		16	16
Gary WATTS (Ducati)	20																					11	9				
James EDMEADES (Kawasaki)	10																					10					

2005 British Superbike Manufacturers Championship
Points after final round

Name	Total	R1	R2	R3	R4	R5	R6	R7	R8	R9	R10	R11	R12	R13	R14	R15	R16	R17	R18	R19	R20	R21	R22	R23	R24	R25	R26
Honda	558	25	25	25	25	25	25	25	20	25	16	25	20	25	25	25	25	13	25	13	16	25	25	20	16	13	16
Ducati	533	20	16	16	20	16	16	20	25	16	25	16	25	11	16	20	25	25	20	20	25	20	20	25	25	25	25
Kawasaki	295	16	9	8	11	20	20	11	11	4	10	11	13	13	9	7	10	11	11	16	9	11	9	13	10	11	11
Suzuki	254	7	8	9		11	8	8	13	11	8	3	5	9	10	16	13	16	8	9	10	16	16	11	11	16	2
Yamaha	187	11	11	11	13	13	6		5	9	2			1	4	6	9	7	6	25	13	9	10	8	1		7

2005 British Supersport Championship
Points after final round

Name	Total	R1	R2	R3	R4	R5	R6	R7	R8	R9	R10	R11	R12	R13
Leon CAMIER	202	13	25	25			20	25	25	13	16	20	9	11
Craig JONES	189	16	13	16	13	20	16	16		20	13	13	13	20
Stuart EASTON	161	20	20	9		11	25	20		10		10	11	25
Cal CRUTCHLOW	161		9	13	20	13		16	16	16	25	25		16
Pere RIBA	155	11	8	8			16	10	10	20	25	11	11	25
Tom SYKES	119		7		20	25	25	13			16			13
Jamie ROBINSON	112	6	10	11		9	11	13	13	11		9	10	9
Jay VINCENT	91	25	16	10						6	8	6	20	
Eugene LAVERTY	84	10		6	4	10		11	7		10		16	10
Simon ANDREWS	67		6	4				7		8	20	7	8	7
Rob FROST	57						9	9	11	7	9	4		8
Kieran MURPHY	53	8	11		11	7	6	5	2		1		2	
Tom TUNSTALL	50	9					7	6	10	4	5	2	1	6
Steven NEATE	48	4	2		6	5		4	5	5	6	3	3	5
Paul YOUNG	37	5	5		16				4					
Matt LLEWELLYN	33						6		8		4	8	7	
Sam OWENS	30		3		2	8	8		9					
Luke QUIGLEY	23	7	1	5		10								
Martin JESSOPP	21								6	3	3	5		4
Craig SPROSTON	20			5	2	5			3				4	1
Gary JOHNSON	20		3		3	3				1	2		5	3
Julien DA COSTA	16									9	7			
Lee DICKINSON	14	1		1	2	4							6	
Andy WEYMOUTH	11	2			4	2	1		2					
Paul SHOESMITH	9				9									
Paul SEWARD	8				8									
Lee LONGDEN	8				7		1							
Steve ALLAN	7	3	4											
Neil MacQUEEN	3				3									
Torquil PATERSON	3							3						
Bob GRANT	2							2						
Joe DICKINSON	2													2
Darren COOPER	1				1									
Allan O'CONNOR	1					1								
Anthony COOPER	1								1					
Pete SPALDING	1													

2005 Metzeler National Superstock Championship
Points after final round

Rounds: R1 Round 01 Brands Hatch Indy 28 March 2005 · R2 Round 02 Thruxton 10 April 2005 · R3 Round 03 Mallory Park 24 April 2005 · R4 Round 04 Oulton Park 2 May 2005 · R5 Round 05 Mondello Park 15 May 2005 · R6 Round 06 Croft 5 June 2005 · R7 Round 07 Knockhill 26 June 2005 · R8 Round 08 Snetterton 10 July 2005 · R9 Round 09 Silverstone 21 August 2005 · R10 Round 10 Cadwell Park 29 August 2005 · R11 Round 11 Oulton Park 11 September 2005 · R12 Round 12 Donington Park 25 September 2005 · R13 Round 13 Brands Hatch GP 9 October 2005

Name	Total	R1	R2	R3	R4	R5	R6	R7	R8	R9	R10	R11	R12	R13
Lee JACKSON	194	13	20	20	20	16		6	5	16	25	20	13	20
Paul YOUNG	166	8		25	25	20	25	25	11	2	3	13	5	4
Adrian COATES	165	11	25			11	20	1	25	25	20	16	11	
Craig FITZPATRICK	152	16	8	16		9	11	16	9	13	11	10	8	25
Ollie BRIDEWELL	124	6	7	7	7		13	11	20	20	16	4	4	9
Les SHAND	110		3	8	11	8		20	8	9	8	25	10	
David JOHNSON	84	10			11	16		16	10	10	2		9	
Ryan RAINEY	83	9	9	10	8	13	6	8	13	7				
Peter HICKMAN	81		6	5	9	3	1	7	4	6	13	8	3	16
Kelvin REILLY	78		7	11	9			10	9			4	11	6
Andy TINSLEY	76	25	16			10	25							
Ian HUTCHINSON	67			3	4					6	7	9	25	13
Aaron ZANOTTI	60		5	4	3	2	4	4	16	5	5		2	10
Steve ALLAN	46								10		11	10	7	8
Marshall NEILL	43	3		13	6	7					8	6		
John INGRAM	38					5	9	5	7			7		5
John CROCKFORD	34			13				13	3			5		
Howie MAINWARING	33	20	13											
John LAVERTY	32									3	9		20	
Stephen THOMPSON	31	2	10			2		5				6		6
Guy SANDERS	26	4									4	1	1	16
Denver ROBB	15						4	7				3	1	
Rory ROCK	14			4	2			8						
Craig COXHELL	10						10							
Kenny EVEREST	10	5		2				3						
Steve BOOKER	8		1						2	2	1			2
Victor COX	7													7
Jason DAVIS	6			6										
Alastair SEELEY	6						6							
Damian CUDLIN	6				5	1								
Dan STEWART	4			1										3
Keith AMOR	3							3						
Rob BARBER	2						2							
Stu WILSON	2												2	
Mark DAVIES	2	1												1
Dean JOHNSON	1				1									
Guy MARTIN	1								1					

2005 British 125 GP Championship
Points after final round

Name	Total	R1	R2	R3	R4	R5	R6	R7	R8	R9	R10	R11	R12	R13
Christian ELKIN	197	13	25	25	25	13	7		13	9	13	9	20	25
J. WESTMORELAND	173			10	7	16	13	20	16	25	25	16	25	
Rob GUIVER	168	20	8	16	11	25	11	7	20	10	20	20		
Dan LINFOOT	134	9		20	20	20	20			8	10	11		16
Chris JONES	109					16	7	25	16	25	20			
Kev COGHLAN	99	25	20					25		16		13		
Ashley BEECH	93	4	11	13	13	8		11		7		10	16	
Brian CLARK	87	16	13		8	9		10	11	11			9	
Michael WILCOX	75		16	8		4	10	10	6	8			13	
Bradley SMITH	73	11				11		13		13		25		
Kris WESTON	72	5	5			10	16	6			7	4	10	9
James FORD	53		4	2	3	1	8		7	3	5	5	5	10
Sam LOWES	49			5	5		6	4	5	4				20
John PEARSON	45		6	9		3	5		9		6			7
Tom HAYWARD	41				6		9	5	3	5	4	2	7	
Aaron WALKER	39					9					9	8		13
James WEBB	34	10	7	11		6								
Alex LOWES	33	7	10								16			
Joel NOON	31			4			2	3	4		6	1		11
Daniel COOPER	26						8				11	7		
William DUNLOP	25						4	9	8				4	
Nathan PALLETT	24						2		6	2		3	3	8
Joel MORRIS	22	8	9			5								
Tom GRANT	19		2	7	10									
Matthieu LUSSIANA	11												11	
Matthew KUHNE	11	2	3	6										
Alex GAULT	9	6					1		1	1				
Dean HIPWELL	9										3		6	
Clement DUNIKOWSKI	8												8	
Alex BARKSHIRE	7								2		1			4
Ashley MARTIN	7				2	2		1				2		
Nikki COATES	6													6
Ben TYE	6												1	5
BJ TOAL	6	3					3							
Toby MARKHAM	4				4									
Davy HAIRE	3		3											
Michael SMITH	3													3
Kyle KENTISH	2												2	
Anthony ROGERS	2													2
Benji DAWSON	1	1												
Paul ROBINSON	1		1											
Daniel HARRISON	1			1										
Jon VINCENT	1				1									
Paul DOBBS	1													1

2005 Virgin Mobile Cup
Points after final round

(R5 column: No race at Mondello)

Name	Total	R1	R2	R3	R4	R5	R6	R7	R8	R9	R10	R11	R12	R13
Billy McCONNELL	173	16	11	16	25		25		20	16	8	10	25	9
Brendan ROBERTS	156	4	9	25	20		3	16		10	25	16	11	20
Tommy BRIDEWELL	150	3	7	10			10	25		25	20	25		25
Jon Boy LEE	136	13	4	9	11		20	20	25	11	9	8	10	
Ian LOWRY	128	25	13	11	13		13	11		13	13		16	
Adam JENKINSON	123	10	20	13	10				13	20	16		13	
Mark POLLOCK	119	20	25	3	8		11	7		6	10	11	8	13
David ANTHONY	101		5	8	16		16	13	7		11		9	16
Conor CUMMINS	87	6	8		5		9	9	11	9	6	13		11
James ROSE	67	2	16					1	16	5	7	20		
Daniel HEGARTY	51	11		20	9				6	1	4			
Tom GRANT	49								7	8	5	9	20	
Craig BEGGS	41		4				7	5	8		1	5	5	6
Matthew WHITMAN	40				10			4	10	3	3	6	6	8
Alex JENKINS	34		1	5			2	6	10	4			4	2
Ross WALTER	32		3	1	3		8	4	9			1		3
Michael NIBLETT	25	8	10		7									
Alex CAMIER	25							3	1			7	7	7
Michael ROSE	19	9		6	4									
Steve MERCER	19	7	6				6							
James COX	17											4	3	10
Ben CASTLETON	15		2	2					5				2	4
Christian ATTEW	12	5		7										
Leon HUNT	12						5			2	2	3		
Jimmy HILL	8								3					5
Lance CRONSHAW	6				6									
Tom DEAN	6		1				1		4					
Brendan FAIRBROTHER	6								2			2	1	1
Peter NEWELL	2							2